TENOR SAX

Wicked
A New Musical

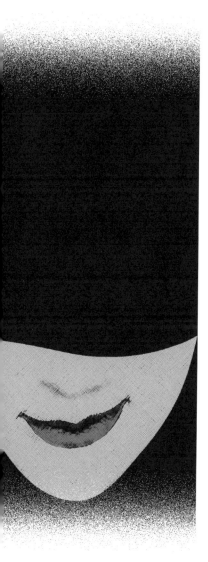

TITLE	PAGE	CD TRACK
As Long as You're Mine	2	1
Dancing Through Life	4	2
Defying Gravity	6	3
For Good	8	4
I Couldn't Be Happier	10	5
I'm Not That Girl	11	6
No Good Deed	12	7
No One Mourns the Wicked	24	13
One Short Day	14	8
Popular	16	9
What Is This Feeling?	18	10
The Wizard and I	20	11
Wonderful	22	12
B♭ Tuning Notes		14

HOW TO USE THE CD ACCOMPANIMENT:
A MELODY CUE APPEARS ON THE RIGHT CHANNEL ONLY. IF YOUR CD PLAYER HAS A BALANCE ADJUSTMENT, YOU CAN ADJUST THE VOLUME OF THE MELODY BY TURNING DOWN THE RIGHT CHANNEL.

ISBN-13: 978-1-4234-4969-0
ISBN-10: 1-4234-4969-X

HAL•LEONARD CORPORATION
7777 W. BLUEMOUND RD. P.O. BOX 13819 MILWAUKEE, WI 53213

Visit Hal Leonard Online at
www.halleonard.com

◆ AS LONG AS YOU'RE MINE

Music and Lyrics by
STEPHEN SCHWARTZ

TENOR SAX

With quiet passion

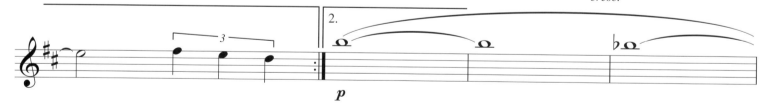

♦ DANCING THROUGH LIFE

TENOR SAX

Words and Music by
STEPHEN SCHWARTZ

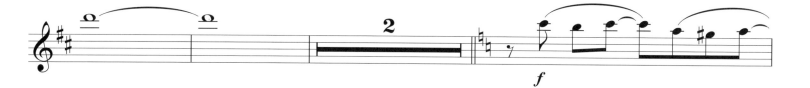

❸ DEFYING GRAVITY

TENOR SAX

Words and Music by
STEPHEN SCHWARTZ

Allegro, as before

Slower

◆ FOR GOOD

TENOR SAX

Words and Music by
STEPHEN SCHWARTZ

Più mosso

rit.   a tempo

senza rit.

mp

rit. poco a poco

rit.   a tempo   rit.

◆⑤ I COULDN'T BE HAPPIER

TENOR SAX

Words and Music by
STEPHEN SCHWARTZ

◆ I'M NOT THAT GIRL

TENOR SAX

Words and Music by
STEPHEN SCHWARTZ

◆7 NO GOOD DEED

TENOR SAX

Words and Music by
STEPHEN SCHWARTZ

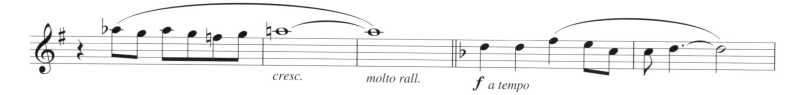

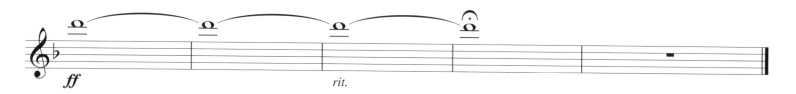

◆8 ONE SHORT DAY

TENOR SAX

Music and Lyrics by
STEPHEN SCHWARTZ

◆9 POPULAR

TENOR SAX

Words and Music by
STEPHEN SCHWARTZ

WHAT IS THIS FEELING?

Words and Music by
STEPHEN SCHWARTZ

TENOR SAX

⑪ THE WIZARD AND I

TENOR SAX

Words and Music by
STEPHEN SCHWARTZ

21

dim. e rit.

Freely

a tempo

mf

Dreamily

mp

3

3

Freely

4/4

rall.

f a tempo

Broadly

rall.

ff

accel.

poco a poco accel.

Bright, triumphant

f

cresc.

molto rall.

ff a tempo

◆12 WONDERFUL

TENOR SAX

Music and Lyrics by
STEPHEN SCHWARTZ

rit.

Moderate Ragtime

f

A little slower

rit. *mp*

molto rit. *f a tempo*

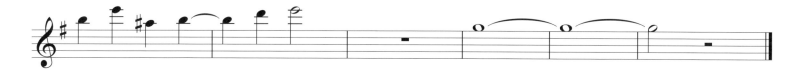

◆13 NO ONE MOURNS THE WICKED

TENOR SAX

Words and Music by
STEPHEN SCHWARTZ